How to use this book

There are important activities which will help prepare your child for reading the story. When he or she has read the story, there are further activities which will help reinforce what has been learnt.

⭐ *Have fun talking about the pictures.*

⭐ *Encourage your child to read the engaging stories again and again for fun and practice.*

⭐ *Use the Star checklist on page 3 to build your child's confidence as he or she colours in a star after each activity.*

Six steps for reading success

1 Practise reading the Speed sounds before each story.

2 Read the Green and Red words before each story.

3 Read the story.

4 Re-read the story to reinforce meaning.

5 Answer the questions about the story.

6 Practise reading the Speed words.

Give your child lots of praise and encouragement. Have fun!

Run run run!

I can read the Speed sounds.

I can read the Green words.

I can read the Red words.

I can read the story.

I can answer the questions about the story.

I can read the Speed words.

Say the Speed sounds

Consonants

Ask your child to say the sounds (not the letter names)
clearly and quickly, in and out of order. Make sure
he or she does not add 'uh' to the end of the sounds,
e.g. ' f' not 'fuh'.

f	l ll	m	n	r	s	v	z	sh	th	ng nk

b	c k	d	g	h	j	p	qu	t	w	x	y	ch

Each box contains one sound.

Vowels

Ask your child to say each vowel sound and then the word,
e.g. 'a' 'at'.

at	hen	in	on	up

Read the Green words

had	fat	man	ran	from
stop	just	past	in	van
that	till	pram	run	

Read the Red words

gingerbread   the   away   said

he   to

Run run run!

Introduction
Have you ever eaten a gingerbread man?
In this story the gingerbread man runs away.
Do you think Dan will catch him?

Dan had a big,
fat gingerbread man.

The gingerbread man ran away from Dan.

"Stop, stop!" said Dan
to the gingerbread man.

But the gingerbread man
just ran and ran.

He ran past a cat . . .

and a man in a van.

"Stop!" said the cat,

and the man in the van.

But the gingerbread man
just ran and ran.

"Run, Dan, run!" said the man in the van.

"Run and get
that gingerbread man."

Dan ran past the cat

and the man in the van.

Dan ran till he got to
the gingerbread man.

But the gingerbread man got on Fran's pram.

"Yum!" said Fran.
"A gingerbread man!"

"Yum, yum, yum!"

Questions to talk about

Ask your child:

Page 7: What did the gingerbread man do?

Page 10: Who did the gingerbread man run past?

Page 16: Why did Dan run after the gingerbread man?

Page 20: Why did Fran say 'Yum, yum, yum!'?

Speed words

Ask your child to read the words across the rows, down the columns and in and out of order, clearly and quickly.

man	fat	stop	run	past
yum	got	cat	to	the
just	ran	pram	said	but
on	get	till	that	he

Help your child to read with phonics

Series created by
Ruth Miskin
Stories by Cynthia Rider
Illustrated by
Tim Archbold

Published by
Oxford University Press
Great Clarendon Street
Oxford OX2 6DP

ISBN 9 780192 733924

10 9 8 7 6 5 4 3 2 1

Printed in China by Imago